THE
PURPLE HARE'S
GUIDE
TO INSPIRATIONAL WRITING

Anne Sheppard

Please visit www.inspiredtowrite.co.uk for contact details

ISBN 978-1-78222-737-3

Copyright 2020 Anne Sheppard

Book design, layout and production management by Into Print
www.intoprint.net
+44 (0)1604 832149

For my children Harry and Georgina
With love

Acknowledgements

My thanks to Keith Westmancott and his wife Annie for their continued support and instruction in all things spiritual; and to my fellow circle members for their friendship and encouragement.

Thanks to Shirley and Phil for reading some of the early chapters and for suggesting I include a chapter on consciousness.

A big thank you also to Craig Hodge for designing the logo and the book covers and for building the website for me.

And finally thank you Michael, I could never have done this without you.

CONTENTS

The Purple Hare's

INTRODUCTION

We are drawing ever closer to the New Age when man will take a great leap forward on his evolutionary journey; when enlightened Homo Sapiens will begin their transformation into Homo Luminous.

Twice yearly at the time of the solstice, hundreds gather at the great stone circles around the world – they gather to witness the sun rise and to witness the slip should it take place – that astronomical slip that will move us out of Pisces and into Aquarius.

While we wait for that new age to begin we are already able to learn and grow by connecting with the universal energy. We can connect through meditation, but the greatest tool that we have been given is the ability to connect through inspirational writing. In modern tech speak it is the way to download from the universe; it is a channel through which we can learn and grow spiritually – something that our spiritual helpers want us to do; they want us to be prepared for what is to come with that new dawn.

The theme of the messages I receive suggests that there is something big going to happen soon. They foretell of blinding shafts of light, of raging fires and judgement, and tell of a new generation born to take man forward; from what I understand some members of this new generation are already with us, and come ready armed with the knowledge needed for this new age.

The purpose of this guide is to encourage you to experience inspirational writing for yourself and receive messages directly. I hope that you will also share what you learn with others and so help spread the word.

We live in exciting evolutionary times and through inspirational writing I believe that we can open the doorway to the next stage in man's journey towards enlightenment. So prepare yourself to be part of that journey and above all enjoy your writing.

1.

What is Inspirational Writing?

Inspirational writing is the Universe's gift to us all; it differs from creative writing because although it is certainly creative it does not use conscious thought. Creative writing uses the writer's thought process, and the writer will usually add to, delete and amend the writing in several edits before being happy with the finished article. Inspirational writing is never altered, it is what it is.

Another kind of writing that is well known in spiritual circles is automatic writing – this involves a spiritual connection; one that is channelled through a medium's body, usually while they are in a trance state. This spiritual link controls the medium's hand and causes the pen they are holding to move and write, with varying degrees of success. It is best explained by likening it to the Ouija board as it works in much the same way.

Free writing is something that writers employ whenever they hit a brick wall or experience writers block. Poets will use it to pull words together. Free writing will often focus on a word or a phrase in order to encourage the mind to go into free fall word association. For example, tree is to forest, is to green, is to leaf, is to autumn, is to bonfire, is to smoke etc.

As I said earlier, inspirational writing is never altered it is what it is. It comes when our thought process is put aside, when our mind is empty but still alert. Some years ago magic eye paintings were very popular; in order to see the hidden picture one had to focus through the painting rather than looking directly at it. In much the same way with inspirational writing we have to focus through our empty mind to see and hear the messages that the universe has waiting for us.

Inspirational writing is something that anyone can do. We are all equal in spiritual terms; age is no barrier, educational level is no barrier, status is of no consequence. For anyone who cannot physically write for whatever reason, then speaking the words into a Dictaphone or app on a mobile phone is the answer. I would say, however, that this should only be used as a last resort and I explain why in a later chapter.

2.

The Purple Hare

The title for this book *The Purple Hare* came to me as I was sitting quietly writing down a list of possible chapters, and mulling over how and where to begin. In amongst my thoughts two words suddenly floated into my consciousness and I wrote them down. The two words were purple and hare and I accepted them as being of relevance to what I was doing at that moment and the more I thought about them the more I realised that *The Purple Hare* would be the perfect title for this guide.

Hares are truly amazing creatures that feature largely in many cultures around the world, including Celtic and Irish folklore and mythology. Traditionally linked to the moon – with the keywords of abundance; balance; fertility; rebirth; transformation and intuition they are regarded as magical, mysterious creatures with supernatural powers.

In animal symbolism the hare is associated with the Goddess Ostara, the Saxon Goddess from whose name we get the word Easter. Easter is celebrated with festivals to celebrate fertility, re-birth and renewal; in paintings

11

Ostara is often featured holding a hare or depicted as having a hare's head and shoulders. The hare is also associated in mythology, magic and symbolism with the Archangel Gabriel, both being linked to the moon and to the carrying of messages.

In Celtic folklore and in the mythology of many regions of the world the hare is also associated with the Otherworld – that world where powerful Gods dwelt and where women shape-shifted into the form of the hare in order to move around on the earth. Because of the belief that the hare was a young woman in disguise, the eating of the hare became a taboo – a taboo that exists even to this day in many parts of the world. In Native North American culture the hare is revered as a Power Animal, a Totem that is associated with magic and the ability to walk between worlds, and whose wisdom includes receiving hidden teachings and intuitive messages. As a Power Animal you can choose none better than the hare in your pursuit of inspirational writing.

Hares are fast movers and can be very difficult to catch; but they also love to lie in the long grass and snooze in the warmth of the sun. You will discover as you learn more that such is the manner of inspirational writing – one minute you are resting quietly, at peace, reflective, and then a second or so later you are racing; scribbling fast, trying to write down the words as they come rushing into your mind like a river in full flood, until you finish, exhausted at the end.

Having explored the significance of the hare I wondered why the hare should be purple; this remained a mystery until I began to explore the spirituality of the subject.

Later on in this guide I explain in more detail about chakras, what they are and how they are used in meditation and visualisation, but for the purpose of exploring their connection with purple I will touch briefly on just two of them for now, the brow chakra and the crown chakra. These two chakras, vital in connection to the universal energy and to receiving inspirational messages both pulsate to the colour purple – the brow chakra to indigo, which is a deep bluey purple, and the crown chakra to violet, a deep rich purple.

Throughout the history of the peoples of the earth the colour purple has been associated with nobility and royalty. Throughout prehistory and in the ancient world, Tyrian purple was associated with the imperial classes of Rome, Egypt, Persia and beyond.

I was fascinated to learn that the dye for the purple cloth was outrageously expensive to obtain because it was only found in a small mollusc that lived in one small area of the Mediterranean Sea. According to the research I have done 9,000 of these molluscs were needed to create just one gram of dye. For that reason it became a colour synonymous with wealth, royalty, power, holiness and nobility – in fact Queen Elizabeth I was so concerned with the cost that she forbade anyone other than close members of the royal family from wearing it.

The rarity of purple dye continued until 1856 when an 18 year old English chemist William Henry Perkin accidently created a synthetic purple compound while attempting to synthesize quinine. He had the good sense to patent the dye and made a fortune in the process. That one small moment in history changed the world of fashion forever; common man could now dress in the royal colours!

With the purple hare as my totem, guiding my hand as I write, I hope to encapsulate everything necessary for you to be able to achieve truly inspirational writing of your own.

3.

My Story

For you to understand my passion with inspirational writing I need to tell you about how and where it all began.

Some years ago when the last of my children left to go to University I re-kindled an interest in spirituality that had begun in my twenties. I joined a local Christian Spiritual Church and through the church I learned about spiritual healing and became a spiritual healer myself. This led to me studying Reiki to level III (Master). I also regularly attended workshops where I learned about the tarot; crystals; dowsing; shamanic healing; mediumship and the auric field among others.

I had heard of inspirational writing and was curious about what it entailed, but had never encountered it personally until I visited a new spiritual group; it was there one evening that I had the opportunity to put my interest to a more practical application.

The group held a weekly open circle – these can be found quite easily by enquiring at mind, body & spirit events, or searching the internet, as many of them have a website or a group page on Facebook. There is another type of circle – a closed circle. Closed circles are where a small number of up to the same 6 to 10 people meet regularly in order to develop their skills in various aspects of mediumship; tarot reading; dowsing; psychometry, inspirational speaking, etc., these are usually held in private in someone's home and are not at all sinister as I have heard some people suggest. The point of having a closed circle is that the group members can feel comfortable working with people they know and trust.

If you are looking to make friends and join a group, then mind, body and spirit events are good places to start. If you have never been to one you are in for a treat, for as well as a multitude of things to buy there are therapists where you can indulge yourself in a variety of holistic therapies and there will also be the opportunity to have a "reading" from one of the visiting Mediums.

Many people believe that anything New Age or connected with mind, body and spirit is pagan; this is not the case at all. Spirituality covers many beliefs and you will find them all at a mind, body and spirit fair – many are Christian, selling angel cards, crucifixes, figurines, dream cards and bible texts; you will also find tarot cards; crystals; fossils; wands; essential oils; pagan artefacts; Buddhist temples and figures; Tibetan flutes and music; Native American beads, dream catchers, jewellery and feathers;

Inuit carvings; Peruvian pan pipes and everywhere incense burning and haunting music playing. There is great diversity but one thing links them all – their spiritual belief and their affinity with the universal energy, nature and Mother Earth.

On my first visit to that particular open circle the evening began with a prayer and then each person stood in turn, to read out loud a piece of "inspirational writing" that they had written at home during the previous week. I discovered that this was the regular format of the evening, and so in the weeks that followed I did my best to produce something "inspirational" to read out – this was no easy task as there was no help or guidance from the group, and no clue to be found searching online, as to what defined "inspirational writing."

As time passed I realised that the inspirational writing in our group took many forms. Some wrote words of wisdom, others words of warning. There were words of encouragement and there were random sentences that seemed to have no meaning. Other sentences were poetic and often dreamlike. Angels and devils were mentioned and colours and situations described. My own writing varied each week and in the early days it took the form of messages that we could all understand. Later it changed and I began to receive a lot of disjointed phrases that I struggled to make sense of. Later still the messages returned but their tone had changed. I have included some examples of these in Chapter 4.

The other members of the circle read out their pieces with a varying degree of confidence. As an inexperienced writer, overjoyed to be receiving anything at all, I felt that some of the pieces I was hearing were shallower than others. These were the messages that focused more upon the writer; offering reams of praise and encouragement. That alone shows me now how little I understood inspirational writing and how I would have benefitted from having a guide like this to call upon.

There was one moment in time during the early period of my writing when I became aware of a fascinating fact: This was something that I found so incredible that I shared it with everyone I thought would be interested. The incredible fact was this: the four greatest philosophers of all time lived and died within 100 years of each other: in Greece – Plato, Aristotle and Socrates and in China – Confucius. Many of us will have heard of these four great men, but the fact that they all lived, wrote extensively and lived and died within 100 years of each other really made me think. That in turn made me smile because what is philosophy if it isn't about thinking?

For a few months afterwards I read and researched philosophy and about the great minds who contributed to the debate that still continues. The classic questions asked and still unanswered: Who are we? Where do we come from? How was the earth built? What's at the end of the Universe? Is there a God? Do I have a soul, and if so where is it? The list is endless and the subject fascinating.

Some of the questions raised by my philosophical thinking are pertinent to the subject of inspirational writing – for example, where do the words come from that I am inspired to write? The answer to that is complex but this does not stop me putting forward my own theory and I talk about this in the last chapter.

Having delved a little into philosophy I got to thinking about other great pioneers from history; were there other periods I wondered where the timescale of achievement was condensed in the same way that it was with the Great Philosophers? I was amazed to find that throughout man's modern history this type of breakthrough in one form or another has repeated itself a number of times.

In art the period known as The Italian Renaissance produced artists and sculptors of a calibre not seen before or since in such numbers: Leonardo da Vinci; Michelangelo; Titian; Donatello; Bellini; Raphael; Botticelli to name just a few of them – contemporaries, living and working in Rome, Florence and the other great Italian cities during the 15th and 16th centuries.

In music the 18th and 19th centuries was the period of the great composers: Beethoven; Mozart; Tchaikovsky;

Chopin; Bach; Brahms; Haydn; Schubert etc. the names go on and on, in fact almost every so called "great" composer was born and lived, or lived and died during that period.

The list continues with great strides forward over relatively short time spans, To mention just a few: – in science (Einstein, Newton) in medicine, (Fleming, Curie), in engineering (Brunel, Stephenson) in technology (Bell, Franklin) they each had their Eureka moment! It is important to realise though that these great men and women did not experience their "light bulb awakening" while reading a book, for what they discovered had never been written about – no, their moment of enlightenment was essentially a spiritual one.

Now at the beginning of the 21st century is spirituality poised to make its mark on mankind, is our Eureka moment imminent?

In the next chapter we will begin to do some writing but for now I will leave you with a quotation from Alfred Lord Tennyson that seems particularly relevant at this time.

> *For words, like Nature, half reveal*
> *And half conceal the Soul within*

4.

Starting to Write

Before starting to write it is helpful to set the scene – especially so while you are becoming familiar with the different aspects of inspirational writing.

Firstly ensure that you won't be disturbed; put a note on the door if necessary and turn off any phones. Light a few candles, burn incense or essential oils, (sandalwood or frankincense work well), dim the lights, play some music, do whatever enhances your connection to spirit and makes you feel comfortable. During inspirational writing we open ourselves up to the universal energy and so finding a safe and peaceful place to do this is very important.

Inspirational writing does not have a magic formula for success; there are no hard and fast rules, but there are ways to enhance the experience and encourage the flow of energy which in turn encourages the flow of words. That first time sitting down and waiting for "something" is like offering a key up to the lock and wondering if it is the right one for the door. It will be, but whether the door opens a fraction or flings itself open wide is for you to discover.

Through experimenting I have found that meditating for 15 minutes or so before writing improves the experience and flow of words – I explain this more fully in the chapter on Meditation and Visualisation. I have also found that if I have difficulty in connecting to the energy or with the flow of words, that using a crystal helps – I explain more about how this works and how to go about choosing which crystal in the chapter on Crystal Helpers.

The very first and most important thing one needs to understand with inspirational writing is that you must go with the first thing that comes into your head, however strange or silly it might seem. Keep focused and keep writing as long as the words keep flowing.

Writing for the very first time is an adventure – opening that unlocked door, not knowing what is on the other side; is it a cosy sitting room or a leap into the dark, or is it something in between? Gather your paper and pen and prepare to enjoy the experience.

Exercise 1

Having carried out your preparation and meditated for 15 minutes you should be relaxed, open and sitting in a peaceful and safe place. Sit there quietly with paper and a pen or pencil in front of you.

Empty your mind as best you can and look down at a spot a little beyond the top of your empty page. If your mind wanders to daily things bring it back to the blankness of the empty page, if nothing comes then ask the universe for some inspirational words.

Once the words begin to flow write them down, keep writing don't try to analyse or correct anything. Don't worry about what it is you are writing or how disjointed or silly it might seem, your writing doesn't need to be too neat either as you can re-write it later. Keep writing until you feel a natural urge to stop.

Now read back what you have written, read it as it is written, don't make any corrections or alterations (except to spellings and basic punctuation) – is it gobbledegook or are there words and phrases that make sense? Does it read as a whole piece or as random unconnected sentences? Remember that this is your first time so don't be too critical if you have achieved little because you will get more with practice. Whatever you have written keep it, don't be tempted to throw it away no matter how little or how meaningless it seems to be at the time. Write the date on the back and then archive it for now.

As I mentioned earlier, it was on my first visit to the open circle that I discovered the group began the evening by saying a prayer and then reading out a piece they had written at home that they called "Inspirational Writing." I hadn't come across this in practice before so I was interested to give it a go. I was given no guidance by the group and so I searched online for information thinking that there would be pages and pages of instruction – I found nothing that satisfied my curiosity and so the following week a couple of evenings before the meeting I meditated for a short time and then sat down pen poised over the paper and let my mind go blank as I assumed one did; having received no instruction it was rather like writing in the dark. Nothing happened for a while and my mind began to wander, so in my head I talked to myself saying something like "come on then let's have something inspirational to write about." Suddenly a phrase popped into my head and I began to write – here it is, that very first piece written exactly as it came without alteration.

"At the bottom of a well you would expect to find water, but that isn't always the case. In a person's heart you would expect to find love, but again that isn't always the case. With a well if you dig a little deeper you are likely to be rewarded with water but the same cannot always be said of love and a seemingly loveless heart. The water in the well doesn't come from rain falling directly into the well it comes from the rain that has fallen around. It feeds down into the well and then lies there in a pool at the bottom. For a heart to contain love it needs to be fed in much the same way as the well, from the love that is surrounding it. For a heart to contain love it needs to

have received love – this is why it is so important to surround with love the seemingly unloved and unlovable!"

I was amazed with what I had written and very surprised by the way it had flowed without any seemingly conscious help at all. I couldn't comprehend where it had come from and I felt a little confused wondering if I had made it all up!

At circle that week when it was my turn to stand up and read out my piece I felt pleased with myself, even dare I say it, rather smug. In many ways my piece was different as it held a message that we could all understand whereas many of the others had written about their spirit guides and angels who were assuring the writer that they were being helped, encouraged and protected on their spiritual path.

Those of you who are familiar with spirituality or who have attended mind, body and spirit workshops will be familiar with angels and guides. For those of you who have had no connection before with this concept it is a simple belief that we have a spirit guide who is with us from before conception until after our death. For me this spirit guide is best described as the voice within – not only our conscience but also that voice or feeling that causes us to sometimes make sudden and often inexplicable changes in our life or our direction; that internal watchdog that alerts us when something is wrong.

Our personal spirit guide works with other guides who will come close to us when needed. As well as spirit guides there are also angels who surround us at all times and watch out for us. Our spirit guide, other guides and angels can all be called upon and will respond to our call; be it for comfort in times of distress, or for guidance when decisions need to be made. There is no end to the help these guides and angels can give, and during meditation it is possible to feel them physically close and see them with our mind's eye. I explain more about this in the later chapter on Meditation and Visualisation.

The following week I repeated the process and again as my thoughts began to wander I called for something to be given to me and very soon afterwards this came into my head (reproduced here exactly as I wrote it)

"How caring can a society be that "takes care" of its elderly and infirm and yet at the same time removes from them the love and affection of a pet! We have all seen the wonderful new developments going up around – retirement homes; third age living; you name it they've got it covered, but read the small print and you'll find "No Pets." Perhaps it is possible to love a new apartment with its practical wet-room, its pretty views and its communal facilities but what a lonely and unloved place it can be if there isn't a cat around to say hello to in the morning – even if it isn't your cat, it will still welcome

*your caress and show its appreciation. Or a bird in a cage
that needs looking after, and is company with his chirruping.
People living alone need their companions. The love they give
and receive fulfils their life in so many ways, more than a wet
room or a shiny new microwave ever can."*

That piece went down well with the others much as
the previous one had, but coming back to it at a later date
I found myself disappointed by its tone and I wondered
whether I had started off writing inspirationally but that
somehow my conscious mind had taken over. Despite
some doubt I was still interested in writing something on
a weekly basis, but by the third or fourth week I felt that I
was being hi-jacked by some of the others in the group as
I found my writing moving towards the ethereal realm of
angels and the search for encouragement from my guides
and spirits. It is for this reason that I don't recommend
group writing on a regular basis until you have become
confident with your own ability to forge a strong link to
the universe. In a later chapter I talk about grounding and
protection and this can be used to isolate us from any
unwelcome interference.

For several weeks after the first two pieces, other than
encouragement from a host of angels and guides, I didn't
write anything that I thought of any note, but then my
writing began to change and I started to get random
phrases and strange observations. I give you a few extracts

to demonstrate what I mean – all reproduced exactly as they were originally written.

When the spirit rises within look east for inspiration – it will be there if you choose to see.

Resonance is strange; sounds on a beach; why is the sky blue?

Take a look then close one eye, does it look the same? If not don't despair you are the only one who can tell.

Replete after a meal the blackbird sings, the mole deep in his earthy home doesn't hear – but the beetles do!

Each of the above is a stand-alone sentence with a meaning of sorts and though I could find no relevance to myself I did find them inspirational in so far as I thought one of them would make a good beginning for a story or poem. I especially loved the one that begins "When the spirit rises ..." it made me think about the religions of the world and how we look east towards the great religious prophets of the past. I began looking up references on the internet to Eastern religions and felt very drawn to the teachings of The Buddha. For me perhaps the inspiration was given in this way through that one small sentence – a truly inspirational piece of writing in that case.

Before I go into more depth with explanations and

examples of inspirational writing this seems a good place to stop so that you can do some inspirational writing of your own. The exercises that follow are for guidance only, but I recommend that you try them out because inspirational writing is a very personal thing and our body clocks are all different. The time and place does matter and you will notice the difference. Take the time to read and understand, and don't rush! Imagine yourself as a channel where the words can flow, much as water does down a stream: sometimes slowly sometimes as a torrent.

I have always preferred to write using a pad and pen but I don't believe there is any serious reason why you could not write using a computer. I type up what I have written afterwards in order to keep my writing together in one place (I always date and keep the original as well). The only thing I would say about using a computer is that you will come across auto correct prompts and spell check prompts and that could change the flow of the words you are writing. A comma in the wrong place can completely alter the meaning of a sentence so you need to be very careful and aware of this as you type.

Exercise 2

If you have enjoyed doing exercise 1 then I suggest you do exactly the same as before but at a different time of day, and/or in a different location. So for example, if you sat quietly and wrote in the morning, then this time choose the afternoon or the evening. If you wrote in the study try writing in the bedroom, or the kitchen or the garden. Afterwards you can record separately how you felt compared to the previous time. Did you find it easier or harder, did the words flow better or not? Were the words and phrases similar or very different? How quickly did the words start to come this time compared to the previous time?

Each time you write, keep the pieces unaltered and with a date on the reverse, in these early days you can also make a note of where you sat and the time for future comparison. If the pieces are really very scribbly then you may like to re-write them correcting any spellings, but in essence they should be exactly as originally written – punctuation and all.

As you become more confident with your writing you will find that words flow on a daily basis and at random times and places. The exercises above are designed to help you get that flow going and to relax enough to be able to write down what comes without dismissing it as unimportant or irrelevant. By the time you have completed these exercises you should have several pages of writing to scrutinise, so read through what you have written and make a note if you find any of the phrases or longer pieces of writing mean something to you. There could be a memory from the past or perhaps from the future? Is there a message from you to yourself, can you decipher it if there is? Is there something profound among the random words and phrases, or perhaps a warning?

Having looked back over your writing I suggest you read it again but this time with the sole purpose of seeing if there is anything there that inspires you to take it further. Is there the beginning of a story or a poem that is waiting to be written? Is there something that whets your appetite to do some research? If there is then keep these pieces separately so that they can be looked over again more easily in the future. There are endless possibilities and with practice these will become more apparent. One thing is certain and that is that those random phrases are not random at all, they mean something and if not to you now then perhaps they will in time.

These first exercises have been done from scratch and if you have had some success then be encouraged because in later chapters I explain how with the help of crystals and visualisation you will be able to enhance your writing experience and surprise yourself with words and pieces you would never have believed possible.

Inspirational writing is exciting; it is a well, full to over-flowing and no matter how much you take out, the words will keep flowing.

The biggest problem with starting to write inspirationally is belief in oneself. It is so easy to dismiss what has been written as something "made up" – this is very similar to the doubts that many mediums experience when they begin their journey. It is important to maintain that faith, that belief in yourself, and relax in order to allow the flow of energy to bring forth the inspirational words that fill your mind.

If by this time you still find yourself unable to write anything then please ask yourself truthfully whether or not you have had words pop into your head but you have discarded them because they have been so random you haven't felt comfortable writing them down. This does happen but you should ignore the impulse to ignore them. Only by writing down those seemingly random and often obscure words will you open the door so that the words can turn from a trickle to a torrent. Try the exercises again and this time relax and go with the flow! Don't be afraid, no-one is judging you; no-one need ever see what you write. If what you do write consists of words and phrases that don't make sense don't worry, try to enjoy the experience and treat it as just that, an experience – looking back at what you have written a few months later could well bring with it a realisation that they did mean something, did make sense after all!

At this stage you may be asking yourself what is the

point of inspirational writing?

I can only answer that by saying that for me inspirational writing has felt like a big step forward in my spiritual development. I feel that there is much to be learnt by connecting to the universe and that if we hope to find enlightenment then we must do everything we can to hear and share the messages that come our way.

5.

Recording your writing

My first piece of advice is discard nothing! As well as it being interesting to keep a record of one's writing to look back on, you will be surprised how often that sentence or phrase that meant nothing at the time, suddenly "makes sense." This is often the case when you have had time to absorb and reflect upon what you have written. Something happening in the World may trigger a flash of insight. Go back and read through your writing after a month or two and you may read different meanings and inferences into many of the pieces. If you are comfortable with other people reading your ramblings then share them, as their observation may be completely different to your own. Often another person's opinion will trigger a response from you – you may feel that they don't understand at all, whereas you suddenly do!

From time to time I gather up all of my recent writings and type up a copy and generally save them by the month and year. With smaller random words and phrases I type them up one after the other and call them Ramblings (e.g. June 2019 Ramblings) For longer complete pieces I keep them separately but still make a note of the month and the year. Having typed them up it is easy to print them off and keep them in a file and look back and refer to them. It is also easy if you have them in a file on the computer to use the search facility to find a particular piece or phrase. The search facility is also a good tool for finding the same word if you feel that the same one keeps cropping up – by writing down in sequence the phrases where that word occurs a coherent message may be revealed. We are all learning a new language here, the language of the universe and not one of us (yet) is fluent, so look for repetition, or synchronicities, study the code.

Having typed them up I like to keep the original written pieces in a loose file as they themselves make interesting reading; written on all manner of bits of paper – the backs of postcards; birthday cards; envelopes; shopping lists etcetera they are the memorabilia of the future.

One of the main points of inspirational writing for me is the pleasure I get from it. Every time I sit down there is the excitement, the anticipation, the curiosity about what I will write; what phrases will I receive; will there be anything more profound than the last time?

Don't think though that the only time you can write is when you have prepared yourself by being in a quiet place and sitting with a pad and a pen, mind empty waiting for the words to drift into your head. Once you begin writing inspirationally you will realise that words float into our mind all the time, we dismiss them because they arrive inconveniently while we are working or cooking lunch or chatting to someone. You will be reading a book when suddenly a random phrase will pop up and you wonder where that came from. Where indeed? For this reason I try to always carry a notebook around with me but as I mentioned before sometimes that is not possible. No matter how you try, those random words are forgotten almost as soon as they arrive, there is only one way to preserve them and that is to write them down!

In inspirational writing mindfulness plays a part too, because when I sit down with the intention of tapping into that spiritual connection, my mind is focused on the empty space rather than fragmented thoughts of mundane daily life. Mindfulness keeps me focused and by being focused I am able to enjoy the experience. The pleasure of enjoying the moment ensures that I will revisit again and again for the pure joy of it.

Once you feel confident and comfortable in sitting down to write and have begun to understand how the words simply flow through your mind, either mindfully as you call them into the empty space, or randomly as they arrive unbidden, you are ready to move onto the next chapters that explore various ways to enhance your writing and your enjoyment of it.

6.

The Chakra Doorways

Depending upon how much success you have had with your writing already, you may feel that you don't need to read the following chapters with their suggestions of how to boost the energy flow. I would say though, that unless you try, you may never know how that boost could enhance your inspirational writing experience, or discover how much you are capable of.

This is a book primarily about writing inspirationally and so in this chapter about chakras I don't go into any great depth other than to help you understand what they are and how they work. They are a complex subject and many books have been written exploring the meaning behind them – what they are, how they work, how they can be utilised and the difficulties that can be caused if they are not working properly

In simple terms chakras are doorways of vibrational energy that spin, much in the same way that a Catherine wheel spins. Like a doorway they can be open or shut, and can be opened and closed. Like a doorway too if the door is sticking it can cause problems – in chakra terms this leads to an imbalance, a blockage.

There are seven main chakras located at important points between the crown of the head and the base of the spine. Each one has its own vibrant colour and often when meditating or receiving a holistic treatment – Reiki for example – you will find yourself unbidden seeing one or more of these colours behind closed eyes.

The three chakras closely involved with inspirational writing are the crown chakra, the brow chakra and the throat chakra but I will describe them all as you may not have come across chakras before.

At a Mind, Body and Spirit Fair or at one of the hugely popular Healing Festivals that are held regularly around the U.K. you will undoubtedly find someone offering to balance your chakras using either Reiki, crystals or a pendulum. There will be a small charge but this is something that I would recommend from time to time as free flowing energies are essential for a healthy balanced life. The energy that flows through the chakras vary in their purpose and I will try to explain clearly and simply what those purposes are.

The root (base) chakra is situated just below the base of the spine; the fact that it is situated outside of the physical body is not a cause for concern, as it sits within our aura. Aura is simply the name for the energy field that surrounds a person or thing. The colour of the root chakra is red and its energies cover the important issues of safety; grounding; stability; self-worth and good judgement. If this chakra is unbalanced it can lead to a feeling of unexplained anger against oneself; a feeling of being unworthy and unloved; a feeling that nothing matters and of being ungrounded and unaccountable – it can cause a person to take unnecessary risks.

The sacral (navel) chakra is situated just below the naval. Its colour is orange and its energies cover the ability to nurture and be nurtured, this is the empathy chakra; it is connected with the ability to understand and share the feelings of others, it is linked to being flexible and with the generation of new ideas. Being unbalanced will lead to a lack of sexual desire; shame; blocked creativity and self-neglect.

The solar plexus chakra is situated just below the breastbone. Its colour is yellow and its energies concentrate on trust; willpower; drive and decision making. This is the chakra where you get your "gut feelings" from. An imbalance here will cause fatigue; insomnia; lack of ambition; anger and resentment and a tendency to blame others.

The heart chakra is situated in the middle of the breastbone. Its colour is green, although many people also associate it with the colour pink. As one would expect, this chakra is connected to the ability to love and be loved; compassion; sympathy; forgiveness. An imbalance here can lead to feelings of hatred; despair; loneliness; bitterness and jealousy.

The throat chakra is located in the hollow of the throat. Its colour is pale blue and it is associated with the ability to speak one's truth; to be a good listener and to be creative and artistic. If you develop a tickly cough for no apparent reason during meditation then that is a sign that there are words that you need to be speaking (or writing). If this chakra is unbalanced the person has poor communication skills and is unwilling to listen; they are reluctant to join in conversations and if they do then they tend to lie and exaggerate.

The brow (third eye) chakra is situated in the middle of the forehead. Indigo (dark bluey purple) is the colour associated with this chakra. This is where our inspiration; intuition; vision and insight come from and it is the chakra we use to visualise during meditation and where our sixth sense stems from. An unbalanced brow chakra will lead to the inability to learn from experience and unwillingness to allow spiritual awareness to flow, leading to a lack of perception and basic understanding. A blockage of this chakra can lead to a feeling of imprisonment due to the inability to communicate clearly.

The crown chakra is situated just above the top of the head and is associated with the colour violet (purple). Like the root chakra it lies just outside of the physical body. It points directly up towards the heavens and symbolizes purity which is why it is often also associated with the colour white. The crown chakra is associated with faith and spirituality; attachment to the divine; insight and wisdom. An imbalance here will lead to a feeling of confusion; the loss of belief; doubt and arrogance, a feeling of being adrift and lacking any purpose

The colours of the chakras are based upon the frequency at which each chakra spins – this is linked to the colours of the rainbow – the light spectrum. In a later chapter I explain how crystals of similar colours that vibrate at the same frequency can help bring the chakras back into alignment. This is another way to balance the chakras and one that we can do ourselves.

The chakra meridians have been used in eastern medicine for thousands of years; they are used today in the west by acupuncturists to regulate and balance the flow of life energy; to block pain or to bring about pain relief. There are other alternative therapies that work with the flow of energy, for example reiki and reflexology. Both of these are becoming more widely accepted as normal holistic treatments and both are now offered on the NHS to cancer patients and in hospices for the relief of symptoms and stress in end of life care.

I have had my chakras balanced several times by the

use of a pendulum or by receiving a reiki treatment. In each case the therapist was able to tell me which of my chakras were out of balance. After a treatment one might feel a little light-headed but otherwise perfectly normal, the benefit becomes more apparent after a few hours as one feels a lightness of spirit and less tightness in the areas that the therapist has worked on. I always feel wonderful afterwards; relaxed, fluid and ready for anything!

The relationship between the chakras and inspirational writing is the energy flow. If your crown chakra needs balancing then the universal energy will not flow easily. With an imbalanced brow chakra you will find visualisation difficult as this is where inspirational writing starts; with the visualisation of a picture or words. If your throat chakra isn't vibrating easily then the thoughts/words may flow but they are likely to be disjointed and unevenly paced. You may even find yourself with a tickly throat that makes you stop to take a drink of water.

Of course there are millions upon millions of people in the world who have never heard of the chakras and who have certainly never had them consciously balanced. This fact hasn't stopped them if they wished, from writing beautiful letters, stories and poems. Balancing the chakras helps with the outpouring of words it doesn't have anything to do with the manifestation of the words in the first place, only with the flow.

In this chapter I have only touched upon the bare bones of chakra meanings and use – there are hundreds of books and many articles on the internet where you will be able to discover more if you are interested.

7.

Writing some More

From a young age I have enjoyed writing. I used to be an avid letter writer before emails came along and rather spoiled that experience. Receiving an email doesn't have the same sort of zing that a letter falling on the doormat has and surprisingly, or perhaps not, I rarely send newsy, chatty emails any more in place of the letters; instead like a lot of other people I connect through social media. I still send a few postcards when I am away and recently I decided that I am going to try to start writing letters again to my children at least.

Upstairs I have a box of letters that I wrote to my Mother when I left home at the age of 18 – she kept them all and gave them back to me shortly before she died. They span a period in my life from when I went away to college to several years after I married and I love to look back over them – they tell me a great deal about what sort of a person I was in my youth. I have also kept some of the ones that she wrote to me and these are very precious now that she has gone. I also enjoy writing poetry and short stories.

Discovering inspirational writing, which was for me something completely new, came at a good time in my life; my children had left home some years earlier and I had plenty of quiet free time in the evenings to focus on different aspects of spirituality. I enjoyed learning about spiritual healing, the tarot, dowsing and working with crystals, and having qualified in Reiki to level III I began to offer healing at home and at Healing Fairs.

Almost everything spiritual that I have encountered I have enjoyed. I love to meet new people and share ideas, learn new things and discuss our different theories and beliefs. Discovering inspirational writing was, to begin with, just one more spiritual thing, but the more I wrote the more I felt a deep connection with the words that came from nowhere, and my curiosity was aroused.

As I mentioned before I first heard of inspirational writing at an open circle meeting . We would read out our pieces and others would comment and then we would move onto something else. I tried a few times to talk to some of the others about their writing and where they thought the words had come from but it seemed to be a given belief that the words came from spirit. This answer wasn't definitive enough for me – ok, so they come from spirit but which spirit, a particular spirit, or the Divine spirit, or spirits collectively?

I continued taking pieces along to the circle to read out

each week but I was writing more and more at home and the pieces I chose to share were the ones that appeared to have a message or at the very least made sense. A lot of the words and phrases I received were very random and downright bizarre, for example: *"Brown cows have brown eyes. Dragons have red eyes unless they are friendly and then they are green."* That one made me laugh, where did it come from, surely I must have made it up? Thinking about it later though, I wondered whether it was a coded message in the same way that the parables Jesus told were stories with a hidden message, but if so how to decipher it?

The lack of any guideline hindered me a lot in the early days as I was constantly looking online, entering different words and combinations of words into the search. What I came up with were books devoted to encouraging people to be inspired to write fiction, or books for children, or poetry and that wasn't what I was looking for. In fact I didn't know what it was I was looking for because it seemed to be a complete unknown. Dictionary definitions of Inspired brought up among others: – *"Divine influence;"* *"Imbued with the Spirit;"* *"A force or influence."* This made me think of Star Wars – "May the Force be with you!" Yes I thought, this is what I am looking for, something that is outside of me and yet uses the force within.

The more I wrote the more frustrated I became. I felt that I was only scratching the surface and I wanted some guidance to help me dig deeper and find some answers. I talked to a few people but they just shook their heads or shrugged and suggested meditation. I considered hypnosis but quickly dismissed the idea as that route is not for me. I trolled the internet and the online bookshops and found absolutely nothing on the subject so I began to doubt my own belief. These doubts, however, didn't last for long as I sat down one morning and wrote the following piece:

Wilson was seventeen when he died, a goodly age for a family dog, but even though his life was over the memory of his love and loyalty never left my Nana's heart. Old Wilson we children called him, young Wilson is what she remembered and when she joined him several years later we took great pleasure in enclosing his precious ashes in her silk lined oak casket. Together now they lie at rest, a lovely lady and her darling pet.

Wow! – I knew without any possible doubt that Wilson had existed at some point in time and I wondered had he been my dog? Was I the old lady or was I the narrator, the grandchild? Wilson in my visualisation was a grey wire-haired lurcher, something like a smaller version of the Irish wolfhound and my love for him flowed with every word that came. What I didn't know though, was whether the love I felt was a memory of my own love or something that the universe was giving me.

You might be familiar with something known as the Akashic Records. If you've never heard of them it is the name given to an ethereal library, where it has been said, all human events: thoughts, words, deeds and emotions that have ever occurred in the past, present and future are stored. On a personal level it is where our soul records are kept – a record of every moment of our lives throughout all of our incarnations past present and future. There are many references to them on the internet if you wish to learn more.

This piece of writing about Wilson is the kind of memory that if it belonged to me, would be written in my soul memory, in my Akashic Record. Writing about him with all of the deep emotion that came with it caused me to think more about the complexity of inspirational writing and how there appears to be more than one "brand" available.

Our feelings for love, hate, anger and so on are so easy to tap into. Vivid dreams can stimulate such strong emotions that we often wake shaken by the reality of them. This love that I felt for Wilson was akin to that, although I had no conscious memory of him I was able to picture him, smell him almost, visualise his surroundings – the house, the garden and yet the old lady was hazy, indistinct and tantalisingly out of reach.

Rather than increasing my doubts about the source of

the inspirational writing I had been doing, this piece about Wilson reinforced my belief that there was something deep that I was able to touch but only superficially. I was now beginning to realise that inspirational writing comes in several forms – some from spirit; some from our own soul memory; and some from an unidentified source. It was the writing from the unidentified source that intrigued me the most; almost like telepathy I felt the link was there I just needed to make a stronger connection.

Generally the group enjoyed the inspirational writing exercise that we did every week at home. Like me a few others were writing short unconnected phrases, while others were extolling the virtue of rainbows, walking in the fresh air and communicating with Angels. Whatever we wrote and read out we always received words of encouragement, even sometimes for something that I thought personally, was absolute rubbish! I feel ashamed now to remember how judgemental I was, and thankful that I kept my thoughts to myself. Occasionally there would be something different, something that seemed to have a little bit of magic attached to it, a hidden message perhaps, but except for recognizing that it was different I wasn't able to say whether the writer had been inspired or not. Those odd snatches though did reinforce my belief that there is something else, something intangible, and that I wasn't the only one able to tap into it.

By this time I was beginning to enjoy my inspirational writing on a daily basis and would do it whenever I had a quiet moment – perhaps while sitting in the car outside the supermarket, sitting on a chair in the garden or sitting on the edge of the bed just before bedtime. Sitting seems to be the key, for me at least, sitting and relaxing. I began to look forward to those flashes of "inspiration," those moments where I felt compelled to write down the words that came flashing from nowhere. It was an exciting time as every time I began to write I had no idea what I was likely to write about. I just allowed myself to go with the flow and enjoy. Once again I would like to stress that it is important not to change anything, but to write down exactly what you receive. Here are some examples of writing from my early days:

While I am here I can see more than when I am outside – fly wide and high like a helicopter on a mission; downwind and overhead, out of sight and out of mind. Does the wind blow from the north or in a straight line? No-one knows.

The window is open and looks out on the soul of mankind. There is little justice in the world these days. Now we can move forward only an inch at a time. We are standing in quick sand and only the brave and the pure will endure. Judgement is riding his horse over the hill and tomorrow he will arrive and begin showing just how powerful our creator can be!

A long time ago I lived on a hill in Nepal, the ground was stony and we could grow very little but there was a tough little flower with white petals that grew everywhere even in the shadow of the stones. We called it old man's weed but I have no idea why.

When the wind blows through the French doors the black eye closes. I am alone it is dark and where is the white swan?

Walk in the long wet grass, it will invigorate you and give you cold feet. Cold feet are guaranteed to keep you awake so you are sure not to miss the rainbow at midnight.

A dim light in my head and over reaching the beds of reeds and the heads of corn – so many mouths to feed. Toss a coin and see who wins. No-one, nowhere to see the results of this morbid attitude. Who cares anyway – he is such a selfish individual. No going back, no stopping to stare.

Wandering among the clouds on a summer's day. Look up, see the blue and wonder – can they see you? More likely they are watching others more deserving of their time; don't think however that you go unobserved! As night draws in all records are reviewed and deep at night when sleeping sound your daily record will be found. For all of us are precious souls and none more so than you.

I immediately thought of the Akashic Records as I wrote that last piece; food for thought certainly!

These random snippets are different in many ways. Some appear to be narrative, possibly of memory, several are observations while others are truly random and it is these that I look at for hidden messages; where is the white swan I wonder?

Having read this far I am sure that you are ready to sit down and start writing again. The pieces above are examples only but I hope they show you how different the words and phrases can be and how they cover many different styles and subjects. Nothing you write should be discarded – make a note of the date and archive it.

If you did the exercises in Chapter 4 you will now be familiar with your own writing style; with how the words flow and whether there is any particular time or place where they come more easily. I suggest if you aren't already doing so that you carry a notebook and pen around with you and when you have a quiet moment just take some time to relax and practice writing. Allow yourself to go with the flow and see what occurs.

In the next chapter I talk about Meditation and Visualisation which are two of the ways in which you can nurture your writing experience and possibly enhance the results but before then see what you can achieve with what you have learnt so far.

8

Meditation & Visualisation

If you belong to a spiritual group, or mix with people who frequent the mind body and spirit world you will know that meditation is spoken of as the key to everything. There are scores of books on the subject as well as guided meditation cd's and for anyone wishing to take things a step further there are dozens of retreats available both here in the UK and abroad. If you are single and rarely take a holiday because you have no one to share one with then a Meditation or a Yoga Retreat may be the answer as you will find like-minded souls, often travelling alone, and as well as the retreat there will usually be the opportunity for some sight-seeing.

If you are already happy and familiar with meditation then there is possibly no need to read to the end of this chapter, however if you have little or no experience of grounding, of calling the spirit guides and angels to come close or of opening the chakras then please read on:-

- Firstly you need to find somewhere that is comfortable, but not so comfortable that you are likely to fall asleep. I prefer to sit on an upright chair but you choose whatever is best for you; it could be sitting in the garden in a deckchair; sitting under a tree or sitting at the kitchen table, there are many places where you can find a comfortable seat, just go with what suits you. This really is one of the key points to meditation, finding yourself in a comfortable place where you can relax.

• Secondly you need to be in a place where you won't be disturbed, so turn the phone to silent and if necessary put a sign on the door telling anyone else who might be around that you wish to be left alone for a certain length of time.

• Lastly, choose whether you prefer to listen to a CD or whether you prefer to sit in silence.

Meditation is used to focus and quieten the mind and can be broken down into three parts: relaxation of the body; relaxation of the mind and visualisation.

Relaxation of the Body:

If you are used to relaxation techniques and have found one that works well for you then please use that to relax, but please ground yourself first as I explain in the paragraph below.

With your feet firmly on the floor, sitting in your comfortable seat and with the cd running if you have chosen one, the first thing to do before beginning to relax is to ground yourself; this is straight forward and simple and takes just a few seconds.

Close your eyes and imagine that you have roots growing out from the bottom of your feet; these roots go deep within the earth and wrap themselves around a large rock or the roots of a large tree. That's all there is to it, you are now grounded. This is something you can do at any time if you are overcome by a feeling of light headedness or are feeling unsteady on your feet.

Having grounded yourself you can now begin to relax by imagining the earth's energy coming back up through those roots. The energy is warm and you may experience a tingling feeling. You are visualising (imagining) this energy as well as feeling it. As it reaches the feet and legs allow them to relax and feel it as it continues slowly on its way up through the pelvis, stomach, chest, back, shoulders, arms and finally to the neck and head. Allow your tensions to unwind and dissipate so that by the time the energy reaches the top of your head you are sitting with your body totally relaxed.

In this state of relaxation you can now visualise the opening of the violet coloured crown chakra which is situated just above the top of your head and which opens like a lotus flower (commonly named water lily). Opening this chakra will allow the brilliant white light of the universal energy to enter and flow through you.

Relaxation of the Mind:

You will concentrate on relaxing the mind after you have gone through the motions of relaxing the body. There are several methods for doing this and I list some examples below. Experiment and choose the one that suits you best.

- *Chanting* – will raise the energy levels in the space where you are sitting, whether this is inside or out of doors. Gregorian Chants are very popular and available on CD or you could try listening to another favourite which is the Gayatri Mantra – also available on CD. All of these can be checked out on YouTube.

- *Breathing* – following a pattern of breathing and refocusing on the breath is a very popular method for relaxing into a meditative state and it is one that works well for anyone who finds that their mind strays. One of the simplest forms is to think as you breathe in; I am breathing in, and then as you breathe out think; I am breathing out.

You can fit this breathing exercise to match your circumstances at the time; for example if you have been ill you can breathe in health and breathe out pain; or if you are unhappy then perhaps you can choose to breathe in the word positive and breathe out the word negative. The options are endless so think also of other words that you could use to fit the moment.

- *Music* – listening to relaxing music such as the sound of water or bird song is another method favoured by many. If you prefer something uplifting or feel you need to raise your vibration further then I suggest you Google "Sacred Polyphony" and find something that appeals – there is plenty of choice and there is some cross over between this type of music and the Gregorian Chants mentioned before.

- *Silence* – sitting in the silence is a simple and effective way of relaxing and has the added benefit that it can be used anywhere; however in this busy modern world finding absolute silence can be difficult. Using ear plugs helps or you can choose to meditate during the early morning hours.

There are many guided meditations available to buy

as well as many free ones to be found on the internet. For a simple meditation you need do nothing other than sit quietly with your eyes closed and empty your mind of everything. This can be quite difficult if you are not familiar with meditating, and so to help, I have listed below three guided options – these are very similar to those you might listen to on a CD.

Visualisation:

In order to begin this part of the meditation you need to be sitting comfortably with your eyes closed. You will have completed the grounding and relaxation process and will have opened the crown chakra. You will be sitting in the silence or listening to your chosen cd. At this stage it can be helpful to choose a scenario – a place to travel to during your meditation.

I have travelled far and wide in the meditations I have experienced. I have travelled on a magic carpet; swum beneath the ocean waves; travelled deep inside a cave and floated on a cloud to name some of the more exotic. Thinking up a place to travel can be quite difficult if you are new to meditation, and so for this reason I have listed three different scenarios below that may help if you are unable to visualise one for yourself – choose just one.

- Scenario 1 – With your eyes closed visualise

this: You are walking down a corridor; there are doors on either side of the corridor; there is a carpet on the floor. At the end of the corridor is a door; it is your door and you can choose what the door looks like. When you reach the door you open it and enter a room closing the door behind you. In the corner of the room is a chair, a comfortable chair. You go and sit on the chair. There is a blanket nearby and if you wish you can wrap it around yourself to keep warm. At the end of the meditation you would retrace your steps back through the door and along the corridor to where you began.

- Scenario 2 – With your eyes closed visualise this: You are walking across a grass field towards a gate on the other side, the field is full of flowers, the sun is shining and there are birds singing; you walk through the gate and close it behind you. Ahead there is a path, walk down the path until you reach the end where there is a clearing. You find a blanket laid out on the ground; sit on the blanket and enjoy the sound of the birds in the trees and the sound of running water from a nearby stream. The sun is warm, everything is peaceful and you feel completely safe. At the end of the meditation you would retrace your steps back down the path and across the field to where you began.

- Scenario 3 – With your eyes closed visualise this: You are walking on a beach, there is no-one else there; it is in an isolated spot and you won't be disturbed. The beach belongs only to you and the sea birds flying overhead. You find a sheltered spot out of the wind and lay out a picnic rug which you sit on. The sun is warm, everything is peaceful and you feel completely safe. At the end of the meditation you would retrace your steps back to where you began.

Whichever scenario you choose this is where the visualisation process begins but just before you start to visualise you can now, if you wish, call silently upon spirit guides and angels to come close and join you on your journey. You may wish to ask silently for healing help, or advice or insight on a particular problem, or you may be looking for love and companionship. If you find that the guides or spirits come in too close and make you feel uncomfortable then just ask silently for them to stand back a little – and they will. Often their presence is felt in the form of different temperatures; or by the sensation of a light touch on the hair or the body; or by appearing to you in recognisable form during your meditation.

The journey is visualised through the third eye – this is the brow chakra, the one that lies in the forehead, just above the centre of the eyes. With closed eyes you "look" through the third eye (brow chakra) and "see" your journey as it unfolds. You find the place to sit and invite your spirits and guides to join you. You then continue, with eyes closed, to look at what is around you and at anything that appears. It rarely happens immediately, but as your mind begins to relax you may start to see pulsating colours, or shapes or forms. You may find yourself travelling or experiencing the feeling of flight; you may see faces or people around you, you may hear voices or experience feelings of heat or cold. I quite often see colours when I meditate but sometimes I see nothing and just float in a black void where time stands still and I remember nothing.

If you find it difficult to relax and "see things" with your eyes closed don't worry because another aid that can be used is the candle. Focusing on the candle flame will help you relax and filter out the hub bub of the outside world. If you choose to try this method then take a candle and sit it on a fireproof plate or in a candle holder and stand it on a table a few feet away from where you are sitting. This is best done when the room is in semi darkness. Light the candle and then when you are relaxed and listening to the music if this is what you have chosen, concentrate and focus on the flame in the same way that you would look through the third eye – for this kind of meditation you are still able to call upon the spirit guides and angels to join you if you wish but you would not journey anywhere, you would just keep focusing on the candle. Once you become totally relaxed then your eyes may close and a journey may take place. If this happens stay relaxed, and enjoy the experience knowing that you are totally safe and that by opening your eyes you will immediately be brought back to your seat in the room.

You will discover that there are many different ways to experiment with meditation to find the one that suits you best, they will all work but look for the ones that you enjoy because then meditating will be something that you will want to make a regular part of your daily routine. Every meditation will be different and if you do find that you enjoy the experience then there are many books on the subject which will give you further insight into other possibilities.

To summarise:

Choose to focus on a candle or select the scenario of your choice and then go through the motions of grounding; breathing; relaxing, opening the crown chakra, inviting your spirit guides and angels to join you and visualising your chosen journey. When you find yourself relaxed and have reached the place where you will spend some time meditating – be it an imagined beach or room or meadow or some other place, then focus your mind on, and look through, beyond the darkness behind your third eye (brow chakra) to the colours and anything that appears. If you find only darkness don't worry, that is a very good place to be; 15 to 20 minutes is usually long enough although you might find yourself reluctant to come back to the real world as the feeling of well-being can be very compelling. I never set an alarm as some inner body clock always prompts me to retrace my steps back from wherever I have been, back to the chair where I am sitting after 15 minutes or so. As you return to the here and now you should close the crown chakra and reground yourself again by sending down more roots deep into the earth. Have a glass of water close by and drink some of it to help lessen the feeling of light-headedness that often follows a meditation, especially if it has been a deep one.

The use of meditation for inspirational writing purposes is to relax and open the mind in order to allow the words to flow smoothly. Inspirational writing is not dependent upon meditation but I have found that it creates a good calm, relaxed state of mind which is helpful.

9.

Crystal Helpers

I touched upon the subject of crystals earlier and I would like to explain briefly how I use them and how I have found them to be helpful in my writing. There are many books on the subject of which I have several, and there are endless references on the internet for you to follow up if you wish to research this further.

In order for inspirational writing to flow unimpeded it is important that the crown, the brow and the throat chakras are aligned and working perfectly; for this to happen the chakras need to be balanced. Balancing can be done by having a Reiki treatment with the intention of balancing the chakras; or by having someone use a pendulum poised over each main chakra in turn, or alternatively one can balance them yourself by following the simple guidelines below:

All crystals are known to vibrate and by holding them close to the body these vibrations will interact with the energy field of the chakra. As well as being able to balance each chakra individually it is also possible to balance the seven major ones by lying down with the crystals positioned over or close to the chakras in question. This is a simple way to balance the chakras but it is important to choose crystals of a similar colour to the chakras in question.

Crystals can also be used to enhance the meditation experience and are a useful tool if you find it difficult to relax or still the mind. To do this one needs only to choose one crystal – one to which you are drawn at that moment – and hold it in the hand during the meditation. For a more targeted experience you can hold it against your throat; brow etc. or you can lie down with it resting on the area of the body where a particular chakra is located, the one that you feel you are having problems with. For the crown chakra you would lie down with the crystal an inch or so above the top of your head. In each instance breathe in slowly and deeply and relax.

Using crystals to align the chakras and to help with maintaining health is a large and diverse subject; the chakras that relate in particular to inspirational writing are the throat chakra, the brow chakra and the crown chakra.

The colour for the throat chakra is pale blue and there are many lovely blue crystals that one can use. Communication can come in the form of speaking or writing and using a blue crystal will aid the flow of words. A poorly functioning throat chakra can affect all aspects of your communication from writing a letter to being able to communicate clearly with loved ones. Too little throat energy and you will find yourself unable to express yourself; too much and you may find that you talk too much, often without saying anything of importance. Using a crystal will calm the chakra if it is too lively and ease the flow if it is restricted.

The colour for the brow chakra is indigo (dark bluey purple). Often called the third eye this chakra is associated with sixth-sense, intuition and visualisation. If this chakra isn't functioning properly then seeing the words in the mind's eye will become challenging and images are likely to be confusing and disconnected. Choose a dark blue or purple crystal to help reopen the channel and allow the colours and visualisations to appear freely and without restraint, it will also help to quieten the noise from a busy mind.

The colour for the crown chakra is violet and is associated with connection to the source and spiritual enlightenment. An unbalanced crown chakra will lead to a feeling of blockage, a lack of light, a feeling of imprisonment, confusion and loss of belief. A deep purple crystal will open up the pathways allowing the light and the universal energy to flow freely again.

Before using crystals it is important to cleanse them. There are several methods and one of the simplest is to leave them on a window sill where the light from a full moon will catch them. Hard crystals can be cleansed in natural running water or in mineral water or rainwater to which sea salt has been added; use a glass, wooden, pottery or china container – never plastic! Soft crystals such as selenite which are likely to break up or dissolve in water need to be cleansed using the moonlight method or smudging.

To smudge/cleanse crystals you will need to buy a tied bundle of herbs. White sage and sweet grass are the two most commonly used and can be found at any Mind Body and Spirit fair or in shops selling crystals. You light the tips of the bundle from a candle, blow gently to encourage the ends to smoulder and then use a feather to brush the smoke over the crystals a number of times.

When you buy your crystals it is worth making a note which method of cleansing is best for them as that is the first thing you need to do once you get them home. Crystals have been around as long as the earth itself and have a lot of history and energy attached to them, some positive and some possibly very negative! When you first put the crystals into sea salt enhanced mineral, or rain water, (never tap water), you will see that they quickly become covered in bubbles that rise slowly to the surface. Once a crystal has been cleansed it is a good idea to repeat this cleansing from time to time especially if other people have been handling them as they will have imparted part of their energies to the stone.

Buy your crystals from a reputable source as occasionally you may find that they are fakes! This tends to occur more often with the more expensive tumbled stones. You may also come across clear quartz crystals that have been dyed to resemble other rarer specimens. Agate slices are often coloured so treat these as decorative pieces rather than pieces to work with. The faked tumbled stones are likely to give off very little negative energy (bubbles) but this isn't always the case so to be sure always buy from a reputable dealer.

Unless the crystal has been in contact with something extremely negative you will never see the same evaporation of negativity as the first time they are cleansed, – if you do then it is worth remembering what your crystal has been doing and who it has been in contact with!

When I sit down to write I will often choose a crystal and place it by the side of my pad. The energies that flow from crystals are incredibly strong and I am rarely to be found without at least one tucked into my pocket – and I have a little family of them in my handbag.

When I first began writing I also found that burning a candle of the same colour as the chosen crystal further enhanced the energies. I very often still use a candle and a crystal, especially in the evening, as they help set the scene and prepare me for the words that are to come.

10.

Consciousness

I believe that consciousness is the element that defines whether our writing is creative or inspirational. Leave the ego behind and you will be able to write inspirationally. Look for some kind of reward and it will slip away into the dark; lost in that still place, where it waits to be found.

Previously I have talked about the source of the words and where the inspiration comes from to write them. Consciousness is the key and unless one is able to understand what an important part it plays in the whole manner of our lives then being able to write inspirationally may well prove illusive.

Our planet lives and breathes consciousness within a conscious universe. The indigenous peoples of the Earth live in harmony with this consciousness, and through their simple lives, – unfettered by the modern religions and materialism of the world – are able to remain in tune with the universal energies that pulsate on a frequency that more advanced civilizations rarely ever hear.

Evidence suggests that we are evolving towards a more spiritual existence; a step backwards in some respects, to retune ourselves to our origins; but for modern man it is a step into the unknown. Boundaries are being erased, man is beginning to listen to his inner voice and that voice is telling him that life needs to be simpler; life needs to be slower and in harmony with Mother Nature in order to avoid devastation on a major scale. This spiritual awareness transcends the five senses; ignoring our bodies which are mere shells. Our minds are the driving force behind this rising cosmic consciousness, we are on the brink of seeing the bigger picture and yet until we can control our ego nothing will change, we will learn nothing.

NASA and other agencies worldwide spend billions listening to the white noise emanating from outer space. As a living breathing member of the universe, the planetary consciousness of Earth will absorb anything that is there to be heard long before the scientists are even vaguely aware, and that knowledge will be shared through the earth's energies with those that are able to hear and understand. Listening to the voice of our own planet and to the voices within ourselves that we can access through inspirational writing may well be the next step along the evolutionary journey of man.

Consciousness as we generally think of it is something that I don't encourage while I am writing inspirationally. Being in a space somewhere between here and there, wherever there is, seems to be necessary for the writing to arrive unhindered and unfettered by conscious thought. Once I become aware of my surroundings or an outside noise disturbs my flow of words then either the writing changes or it dries up.

I have never tried writing while in a trance state and I have no desire to experiment in that direction as I believe other forces would come into play. Our mind in a trance state would be open for spirit to use for its own purpose and that in my opinion would lack the purity that is necessary in order to receive words directly from the universe.

Thinking about writing inspirationally and linking this with our own consciousness brings all sorts of emotions to the surface. What is it? Is it the same as the mind and if so what exactly is the mind; where is it, is it separate from the body or is it a part of the brain? Add to that the question what is the soul and we have come full circle back to the great unanswered question of all time.

Whilst we may not know what the mind is, unless one lumps it generally under the heading of brain, which won't do at all because it is far more complex than that – we do all acknowledge that it exists and that we have one. That is as far as it goes, because the mind is completely private and known only to the human being within which it resides. This thought of residency within our body or brain allows for open thought regarding its relationship to that other mystical thing – the soul. If the mind resides within our body then does the soul reside within the mind? I have no answers but I do believe that the mind and the soul are not one and the same thing.

I read somewhere that we only use a small part of our brain and that there are large areas lying dormant. This is a mind-boggling thought – why would we have parts of the brain seemingly asleep? The brain is obviously alive yet in a partially dormant state – what trigger or incident is necessary to wake up those sleeping areas? Do our instincts, for example, stem from our minds or from somewhere else? The instinct to pull back from a snake or something resembling a snake is well documented – where did we learn that? Is it residual in our brain matter or in our mind? If our mind, then did the mind inhabit our body at some point after conception, coming complete with a vocabulary of knowledge gleaned from previous incarnations? The answers to these questions are unknown, yet answers there most definitely are – we just need to ask the right question in the right way and it will be revealed.

In some ways inspirational writing mimics the few instances of telepathy that I have experienced; it feels as though a connection has been made and that I need to approach it openly without allowing any of the pathways to close. Rather like looking bug eyed at the magic pictures that I mentioned earlier; we need to jiggle the pathways so that the right one opens up.

I believe consciousness is tangible in that it is real and not something imagined. It is part mind and part soul and wholly belonging with the person whose physical presence it inhabits. In order to bypass the dead ends and the false trails when writing inspirationally it is very important to cast consciousness and the ego aside and write "out of gear" in order to be receptive to the messages sitting up there on the great universal server waiting to be downloaded.

11.

Loved Ones in Spirit, Your Time, Your Space

Getting back to the practicalities of writing inspirationally you should by now be familiar with the process and with the different ways you can enhance the experience. I hope that you are enjoying writing and that you are taking care to archive your work no matter how insignificant it may seem.

With some mindful preparation before sitting down to write it is also possible to make a link with loved ones in spirit or seek the answer to a specific question. The exercises below explain this more fully.

Write a letter to your loved one in spirit:

If your loved one was here now, what would you like to say to them? What do you regret never saying to them while they were here? Think carefully and write it down in the form of a letter. After it is written place it beside your pad where you are going to be writing.

Prepare as normal and during that time focus on your loved one and the letter that you have written. Afterwards sit as you would do if you were doing an unbidden piece of inspirational writing. Silently ask your loved one to reply to your letter and then still the mind and wait for the words to flow. If they are slow arriving then write on the paper in front of you the word Dear, followed by the name your loved one called you.

The first such letter that I wrote was to my father, it told him how much I missed him and how much I appreciated him. The reply I received was not what I was expecting as he wrote about his failings as a parent and how much he regretted being aloof and how he wished he could have been more tactile and demonstrative. He asked for my forgiveness.

Ask a specific question:

Think carefully about the question and write it down. Asking "when will I win the lottery?" is never going to receive an answer! A question worded simply is more likely to receive a positive response than something more complex, for example:

- What can I do to improve my relationship with my daughter-in-law?
- Is now a good time to make a career change?

Asking for encouragement:

Our spirit guides and angels are always close by, and will send us words of encouragement and guidance. This is a particularly good exercise if you are feeling low.

I mentioned before that I often feel the urge to write when I am out and about getting on with life generally. This didn't happen in the beginning but it is something that has become more frequent as time has gone on. When this happens I pick up the best writing materials that are available, sometimes a pencil or a borrowed pen and whatever I can find to write on. This is a make do situation but in the beginning and now by preference, I will choose a pen I feel comfortable with and a pad of paper or a notebook that I love the look and feel of. Anyone who is addicted, like me, to shops like Rymans; Staples or W.H. Smith will understand this feeling – all of those lovely notebooks just waiting to be written in!

Having a favourite pen or pencil and a writing pad or notebook that you are itching to write in is the first step in encouraging the energy to flow and the inspirational writing to begin. Where you might in the past have written down a list of things to buy; a bucket list of places you would like to visit; reminders of things to do, you are now poised to write whatever your source is waiting to reveal.

Finding the right time and place to write is one of the most important components in the early days, I mentioned this in Chapter 4 and I can't emphasise this enough – find your own personal place.

The time of day is important too. Some of us are larks

and the energy will flow more easily in the morning while the owls are still sleepy headed. For the owls the afternoon and evening is the best time. Don't feel disillusioned if you try writing at the wrong end of the day for your particular body clock – you know whether you are an owl or a lark so go with the flow, it is your energy and it flows the way it does because it is unique to you. What is important is that when you feel an urge to write then try to do everything possible to find that space, that moment and let the words come.

If you prefer to write in silence make sure that you have it. If you prefer to have music playing in the background then choose that. If you like to be surrounded by flickering candles, or crystals, then choose that. By now I think you will understand what I am saying – choose exactly the environment that is best for you; choose the time of day; the writing instruments; the ambience. All of these choices will put you in the right frame of mind to write. Your body will be relaxed, you will feel wonderful because there is nothing jarring your energy, it can flow easily and without hindrance – so the time has come – pick up your pen again and write!

12.

Looking for the Source

There are many people who will state categorically that they are not religious but then go on to add "but I am spiritual" I would say that we are all spiritual to some extent, whether we wish to admit it or not.

If some wise person whose opinion you value were to tell you that "you are an old soul" or that your new born child is "an old soul" you will likely nod in agreement; pleased at the recognition. It is strange how so many babies have that all knowing look in their first few months – that unwavering gaze that sees all and leaves us feeling slightly discomfited. Is it a meeting of two old souls and a subconscious recognition?

We all have within us the knowledge of our spirituality. For us in the modern civilised world it is buried deep below the indoctrination of religion, but for many in the east it is not, and for more primitive races, for example the Australian Aborigine or the indigenous peoples of The Americas it is accepted without question. They speak to their ancestors and spirit guides, and accept spiritual guidance and connection to the source as part of everyday life – this is part of their universal consciousness.

We have all experienced moments of déjà vu. – a French word meaning "already seen" and which spiritually is believed to be a sign to you that your Spirit has been in this situation, location or scenario before in a previous lifetime. Science has an explanation for this happening, but of course there is an explanation – it is a physical event! The importance of it is not the physical event, it is the spiritual trigger and whether or not we recognise it.

Over the past six years I feel I have come a long way on my journey with inspirational writing, yet believe there is still a lot to be revealed and I relish the thought of those future discoveries.

Talking with others who also enjoy writing inspirationally and drawing together the threads of what I have learnt has been an interesting exercise and I have come to the conclusion that inspirational writing takes several forms:

What I shamefully rejected at the beginning as shallow messages given to some of my fellow circle members, I now identify as inspirational writing generated mindfully from their spirit guide. The repetitive platitudes; the words of encouragement and wisdom; this was a common theme among several in the group but I understand now that those words of encouragement did exactly that – they were encouraged, they did continue on the path, they did grow spiritually and two I know have gone on to become successful practicing mediums.

The first two pieces of inspirational writing that I ever did, which I reproduced in Chapter 4, I now believe were channelled through me, but originated in the spirit world. The fact that they were such complete pieces and held such an obvious message was an obvious clue that I failed to recognise. I mistakenly believed that I was engaging my conscious thought but I now realise that my conscious thought wasn't capable of such writing – where would the ideas have come from? I am not by nature the sort of person who would have those thoughts, I am not an empath and those pieces came from a spirit who undoubtedly is.

The written pieces I treasure most of all are the bizarre fragments and random phrases that have grown into longer pieces the more I practice. I am certain that there is no connection to spirit with these pieces; neither do I believe there is any input from my consciousness or my own spirit guide. My instinct is that this aspect of writing inspirationally is a direct result of connecting with the universe itself, and that this connection allows us to tap into the past as well as into the future, giving us a glimpse behind the veil of our subconscious. It is possible that these messages – the ones that appear to be in code or at least in language that is difficult to interpret – could be the beginning of the wake-up call that our partially dormant brains have been waiting for. I am eager to explore this aspect of inspirational writing further.

The piece of writing I did about Wilson, the beloved dog who died was a piece that really touched my heart. I still haven't come to a decision on this one. Was it a message from spirit or was it a recollection from my soul memory? I rather hope it was from my soul memory as he really was a lovely dog.

My writing has continued to grow and mature and to demonstrate this I copy here the latest piece that I have written, which appears to offer me encouragement in what I am doing in spreading the word:

Give credence to the thoughts and beliefs of others.
Wash your linen in public and all kinds of evil will fall out.
No words can tell or describe which way the wind of change will come, only you can help the reader understand that they are in charge of their angels and guides, and through them their destiny.
Make a map, use pins and draw threads together to link random thought to another random thought. If it is done properly the result will be a kaleidoscope of ideas, and generosity will follow as one person tells another and the word will be spread.
Nobody knows yet but through you the turn, the click is about to happen – be humble.

I wish you happiness and success with your inspirational writing and hope that you will encourage others to read this guide and spread the word – we are only seeing the tip of the iceberg; there is so much more to discover! I hope too that by joining together and sharing our hidden messages we will break the code and help man take that next step towards enlightenment.

Please visit my website to share your contact details so that I can keep you informed of any inspirational writing workshops that I am running and about any future publications and anthologies.

* * *

Footnote:
If you have a piece of inspirational writing that you would like to be considered for inclusion in an *Anthology of Inspirational Writing* that is planned for the future, please send it via the "Contact" link on my website: www.inspiredtowrite.co.uk

Lightning Source UK Ltd.
Milton Keynes UK
UKHW021146170320
360484UK00006B/338